CREATE AN
ABSTRACT ART

Alix Wood

 Gareth Stevens
PUBLISHING

Thank you to
Davina Cresswell
and Jemma Martin
for their help with
this book.

Please visit our website, **www.garethstevens.com**. For a free color catalog of all
our high-quality books, call toll free 1-800-542-2595 or fax 1-877-542-2596

Cataloging-in-Publication Data

Names: Wood, Alix.
Title: Abstract art / Alix Wood.
Description: New York : Gareth Stevens Publishing, 2017. | Series: Create it! | Includes index.
Identifiers: ISBN 9781482450439 (pbk.) | ISBN 9781482450453 (library bound) |
    ISBN 9781482450446 (6 pack)
Subjects: LCSH: Abstract expressionism--United States--Juvenile literature. | Art, American--
    20th century--Juvenile literature.
Classification: LCC N6512.5.A25 W66 2017| DDC 709.04'052--dc23

First Edition

Published in 2017 by
Gareth Stevens Publishing
111 East 14th Street, Suite 349
New York, NY 10003

Copyright © Alix Wood Books

Produced for Gareth Stevens by Alix Wood Books
Designed by Alix Wood
Editor: Eloise Macgregor

Photo credits: Cover, 1, 5 bottom, 7, 8, 9, 11, 12, 13, 15 top right and bottom, 16 top right and
bottom, 17, 18 bottom, 19, 20 middle and bottom, 21, 23, 24, 25, 27 bottom, 28, 29 © Alix
Wood; 3, 14 bottom, 15 top left, 16 top left, 20 top, 27 top © Dollar Photo Club; 10 bottom
© Dreamstime; 22, 26 © Artothek; all remaining images are in the public domain

Printed in the United States of America
CPSIA compliance information: Batch #CS16GS: For further information contact
Gareth Stevens, New York, New York at 1-800-542-2595.

CONTENTS

WHAT IS ABSTRACT ART?

Most paintings or sculptures are of a recognizable object, place, or person. Artists might paint a beautiful garden, or a person's face, or a bowl of fruit. Abstract art is a painting or sculpture that isn't of a person, a place, or a thing! Instead, artists use color, shape, and brush strokes to express ideas and **emotions** without trying to create a **realistic** picture.

Abstract artists may use blocks of color, like this artist has, to create their art. The choice of colors, shapes and where the artist puts each block is important. Do you like this painting? What does it make you feel?

Meet an Abstract Artist

The Russian artist Wassily Kandinsky was one of the first abstract artists. He loved music, too. He thought colors were like the different sounds made by musical instruments. To Kandinsky, the sound of a cello was a deep blue!

TECHNIQUE TIPS

It can be hard to think what to draw when you are used to drawing "things." Try this. Using a pencil, draw ten dots, scattered **randomly** on a sheet of paper. Using a ruler, join the dots together to make shapes. Join some dots to the four corners of the paper, too. Color in the shapes using colored pencils, felt pens, or paint. You could use lots of **shades** of the same color, or use different colors.

WASSILY KANDINSKY

As a child, the colors of nature amazed Wassily Kandinsky. He loved art and he loved music. In his paintings he wanted to create the same effect a piece of music would have on a listener. He used color in his paintings to show emotion. Kandinsky wasn't interested in making objects look real. He believed that shapes and colors alone could be art. He was one of the **founders** of abstract art.

Part of Kandinsky's work *Color Study – Squares with Concentric Circles*

Kandinsky thought triangles caused aggressive feelings, squares were calming, and circles caused **spiritual** feelings. What do the different shapes make you feel?

6

CREATE IT!

You will need: two large square pieces of construction paper, paints, glue

1 Fold the two sheets of paper in half and then in half again. Open them out. Take one of the sheets. Paint each square with a different color background. You could mix your background colors on some squares like Kandinsky did. Leave to dry.

2 Cut the second sheet of paper into the four squares. Choose the colors you want and then paint a large circle that fills the square. Paint more circles inside that one, getting smaller and smaller.

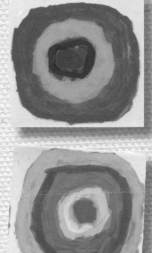

3 Once the paint is dry, carefully tear the square corners off each piece of paper to make them roughly circle-shaped. It doesn't have to be perfect! Decide which circle you want on which background, and glue them in place.

Wassily Kandinsky drew black outlined shapes and lines which he filled with **vibrant** colors. Try listening to or thinking about a piece of music while you create your painting, like Kandinsky did. It may inspire you!

You will need: construction paper, a black crayon, watercolor paint, a paintbrush, a ruler, different shaped objects to draw around

1 Draw lines on the paper using the ruler and crayon. Add some shapes by drawing around objects such as plates, bowls, boxes, pencil sharpeners etc. Add a few wavy lines, too.

2 Using the crayon, add some dashed lines around some of the shapes. Add a few movement lines too, such as small **arcs** around circles, and corner lines around squares.

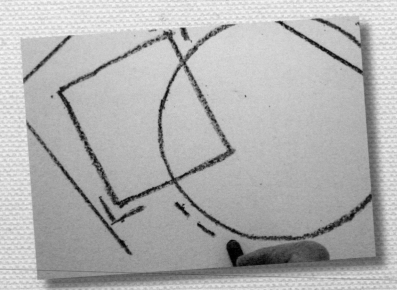

3 Using watercolor, start filling in the sections of the drawing. Try to use two different **tones** of the same or similar color in some shapes. For instance, use yellow and orange and blend the two colors together at the middle.

4 Once the painting is completely dry you could go over your black lines with the crayon. You could add some more squiggles and lines too, if you like.

HENRI MATISSE

Henri Matisse was a French artist known for making colorful works of art. His paintings influenced many abstract artists. Some abstract artists do paint "things," but they don't paint them in a realistic way. Matisse used bold colors and often created colorful, patterned backgrounds.

Matisse's portrait *Annelies, White Tulips and Anemones*

CREATE IT!

You will need: construction paper, pencil, paints

1 Draw your portrait first in pencil. Then paint the face and hair in natural colors. Let it dry.

2 Create a colorful, patterned background. Once the background is dry, outline your portrait in black.

TECHNIQUE TIPS

Make sure you wait for your paint to dry before you put any stripes or dots on your background. If you don't, your paint might smudge.

As Henri Matisse got older he found it difficult to stand at his **easel** and paint. He invented a new technique he called "painting with scissors." He painted large sheets of paper, and then cut out free-flowing shapes. He made beautiful collages by gluing the shapes onto paper.

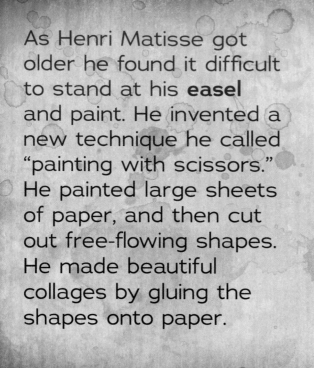

CREATE IT!

You will need: construction paper, pencil, scissors, glue

1 Cut some shapes out of colored paper. If you prefer, you can draw the shapes in pencil first.

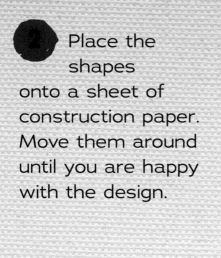

2 Place the shapes onto a sheet of construction paper. Move them around until you are happy with the design.

3 Glue your pieces onto the paper. Remember to stick the ones you want in the background first.

PIET MONDRIAN

Piet Mondrian was a Dutch painter. At first he painted realistic **landscapes**, but gradually his style became abstract. The more Mondrian looked at objects, the more he admired their basic shapes and colors.

Eventually, Mondrian's paintings became simply shapes and primary colors. Primary colors are red, yellow, and blue.

TECHNIQUE TIPS

How do you see an object's basic shape and color? Squint your eyes while looking at something. All the details will start to blur. You will gradually see only shapes and color.

CREATE IT!

You will need: white construction paper, ruler, pencil, black marker, felt pens or colored pencils

1 Choose a colorful object to draw. Squint your eyes and try to divide your object into its different colored squares.

2 Outline the squares using a ruler and a black marker. Color in the squares using felt pens or colored pencils. Just use primary colors red, yellow, and blue, like Mondrian did. You can also use black and white.

CREATE IT!

Piet Mondrian painted **geometric** shapes using bright, primary colors. He often outlined these shapes using straight black lines and white spaces. Try to create your own Mondrian art.

You will need: construction paper, masking tape, thick paint such as gouache or tempera, paintbrush

1 Using masking tape, divide up your paper into squares and rectangles. Make sure the tape is pressed down well, so that no paint oozes underneath when you paint. Don't stick it down too hard though, or it may tear the paper when you remove it.

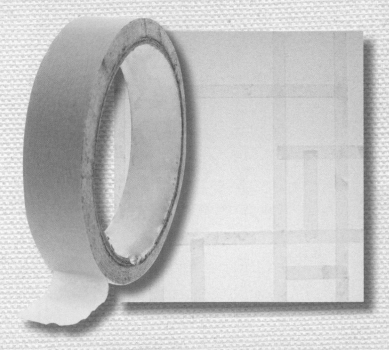

2 Use thick paint in bright primary colors to fill in the squares. It's OK if some of the paint goes over the tape. When you peel the tape away you will be left with a nice, straight edge.

3 As you paint, move across the page from left to right if you are right-handed, so you don't smudge any of the shapes you have already painted. Paint from right to left if you are left-handed.

4 Wait until the painting is completely dry. Carefully peel off the masking tape. If the tape starts to pull off some of the paper, wait a little longer – your paper is probably still too wet.

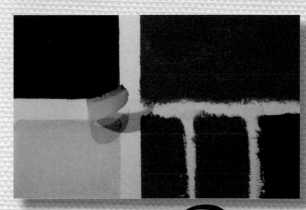

PAUL KLEE

Paul Klee was a German painter. He often painted beautiful patchworks of color. He liked to paint in unusual ways such as stamping or spraying his paint, or drawing with a needle on a blackened pane of glass. Klee often worked using different kinds of paint, ink, and pastel all together on the same piece.

CREATE IT!

You will need: paper, crayons, watercolor paint

1. Draw a town using a crayon. You can draw it using pencil first if you like. Make the buildings all different heights and with different shaped roofs. Add some windows and some tiles.

2 Paint the shapes you have drawn using bright colors. They don't have to be realistic colors. Use your imagination!

The crayon will resist the paint, so don't worry if you paint on top of the lines.

CREATE IT!

A stamp featuring Paul Klee's work _Bird Garden_

1 Draw areas of color on the paper using crayons. Here, we made four red areas for the four red birds, and green and blue areas for the plants. Cover all the paper with crayon.

2 You'll need to remember where your colors were. Using tracing paper or thin photocopy paper, trace the outlines of your colored shapes in pencil. Mark each shape with a dot of its color.

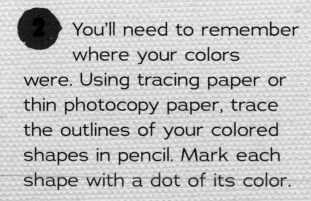

3 Paint black poster paint all over your crayon drawing. If you don't have any poster paint, you can use black crayon, but it does take a lot longer to cover the page.

4 Once the paint is completely dry, draw by scraping away the paint using an opened-out paper clip. Look at your tracing to remember where each color was.

JaSPER JOHNS

Jasper Johns painted *Flag*, below, after dreaming of the American flag one night. He often painted recognizable symbols, such as flags, maps, targets, letters, and numbers.

TECHNIQUE TIPS

Johns used unusual materials when he painted. In *Flag*, he used torn-up newspaper and colored hot wax to create its uneven surface.

CREATE IT!

You will need: newspaper, construction paper, glue, scissors, poster paint

1 Cut or tear some pieces of newspaper. Glue the pieces of newspaper onto a rectangular piece of paper. Try to choose pieces that have writing about your flag's country, if you can.

2 Paint your flag using the poster paint. If you are creating the American flag, paint the blue background and the red stripes first. Leave the paint to dry before you paint the white areas.

3 Once the red and blue paint is dry, paint the white stripes and stars on top.

CREATE IT!

You will need: pencil, paper, ruler, crayons, watercolor paint.

1 Using a pencil and ruler, divide up your paper into 25 squares, with five rows and five columns. You may need an adult to help you. There are 26 letters in the alphabet, but the "I" and "J" are thin, so they share a square! Lightly write the alphabet in the squares, then outline each letter.

2 Choose four colors of crayons and paint to create your art. You could try yellow, blue, green, and red. Color the letters in first using the crayons. Use a little of each color on each letter.

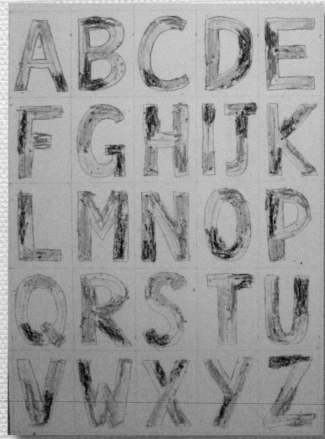

3 Paint around the letters using your four chosen watercolors. Mix up the colors in each square to create a colorful painting.

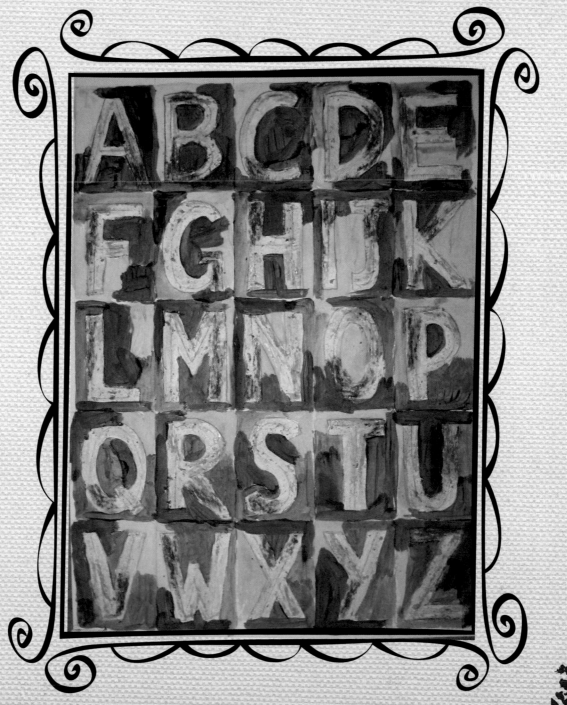

JACKSON POLLOCK

Abstract American artist Jackson Pollock became known as "Jack the Dripper" for his technique of dripping paint onto canvas! He liked to work on very large pieces of canvas. Pollock would lay them on the floor of his **studio** and drip and throw paint to create his art.

Jackson Pollock's Number 16.

When Pollock placed his large canvases on the floor, he would move around all four sides dripping and throwing his paint. Known as "action painting," his style was very new and different.

TECHNIQUE TIPS

Pollock used household paint or car paint to create his art. He put the paint on the canvas using old brushes and sticks. Sometimes he poured the paint directly from the tin. He would place handprints on some of his paintings.

CREATE IT!

You will need: paper, paint, string, an outdoor space, old clothes

1 Set up outdoors and wear old clothes. Dip a length of string into some paint. Lay it on the paper, then lift it off. Try using string to drip and flick some paint. Repeat using different colors until you get a painting you are happy with.

CREATE IT!

You will need: construction paper, paints, a marble, two paintbrushes, a roasting pan or cardboard box

1 Place your sheet of paper in a roasting pan or cardboard box. Half a pizza box works well.

2 Tip some paint into a tray, or a paint pot lid. Roll your marble in the paint.

3 Next, roll the paint-covered marble around the pan.

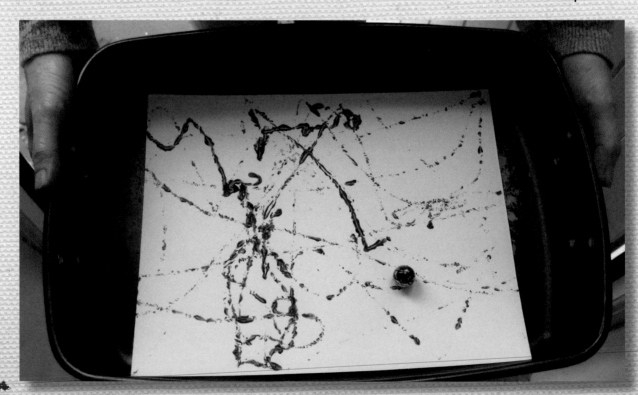

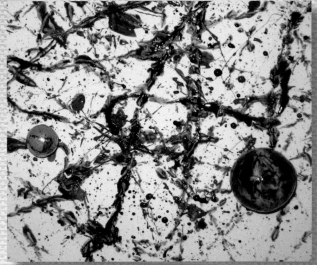

4 Try making some splashes. Gently tap the handle of a **loaded** paintbrush with the handle of another brush. The paint should splatter onto the paper.

5 Try different colored paints on your marble. Keep building up your picture until you are happy with your design. You could try using different sized marbles.

GLOSSARY

arcs Portions of a curved line.

easel A frame for holding up an artist's painting.

emotions Strong feelings.

founders People that establish something.

geometric Shapes such as circles, triangles, or squares that have perfect, uniform measurements and don't often appear in nature.

landscapes Pictures of natural scenery.

loaded Filled, such as a paintbrush full of paint.

randomly Following no clear plan, purpose, or pattern.

realistic True to life or nature.

shades The darkness or lightness of a color.

spiritual Relating to the spirit, or to sacred or religious matters.

studio The working place of an artist.

tones Shades of color or colors that change another, such as gray with a blue tone.

vibrant Having or giving a sense of life, vigor, or activity.

FURTHER INFORMATION

Books

Edelmann, Anja. *Paul Klee: My Art Activity Book Abstract Art*. London, UK: Tate Publishing, 2013.

Rosenstock, Barb and Mary GrandPre. *The Noisy Paint Box: The Colors and Sounds of Kandinsky's Abstract Art*. New York, NY: Alfred A Knopf, 2014.

Websites

Ducksters site with information about famous abstract painters and their work:
http://www.ducksters.com/history/art/abstract_art.php

A FreeSchool child-friendly YouTube biography of Van Gogh:
https://www.youtube.com/watch?v=qv8TANh8djI

Publisher's note to educators and parents: Our editors have carefully reviewed these websites to ensure that they are suitable for students. Many websites change frequently, however, and we cannot guarantee that a site's future contents will continue to meet our high standards of quality and educational value. Be advised that students should be closely supervised whenever they access the Internet.

INDEX

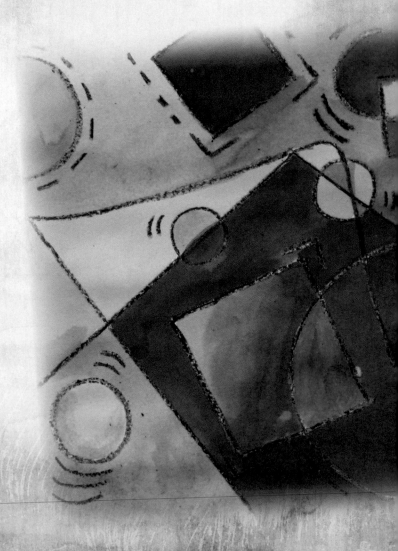